LIVING DEBT FREE

....

Bible Secrets and Prayers to Move From Debt to Abundance

....

By:

DANIEL C. OKPARA

Published By:

Better Life Media.

BETTER LIFE WORLD OUTREACH CENTER.

Website: www.BetterLifeWorld.org

Email: info@betterlifeworld.org

FOLLOW US ON FACEBOOK

1. FB.com/betterlifeworld

2. Join Our Facebook Prayer Group, submit prayer requests and follow powerful daily prayers for total victory and breakthrough

Any scripture quotation used in this book is taken from the New King James Version, except where stated. Used by permission.

Disclaimer

This book is written to provide you with Biblical intelligence, one that I have proven over the years and completely believe in when it comes to debts.

However, these suggestions are general and do not consider specific individual situations. So they should not substitute for professional counseling on investment, savings options, and other financial matters.

God bless you.

CONTENTS

DISCLAIMER 3

CONTENTS 4

RECEIVE DAILY AND WEEKLY PRAYERS 5

FREE BOOKS 6

HOW TO USE THIS BOOK 7

INTRODUCTION 7

(1): WHY YOU'RE IN DEBT...13

(2): THE PARABLE OF THE DEBTOR AND THE CREDITOR 39

(3) WISDOM TO STAY OUT OF DEBT 63

(4): SPEAK TO YOUR DEBTS 76

(5): FROM DEBT TO ABUNDANCE 83

GET IN TOUCH 114

OTHER BOOKS BY THE SAME AUTHOR.................115

ABOUT THE AUTHOR 121

NOTES 123

RECEIVE DAILY AND WEEKLY PRAYERS

Powerful Prayers Sent to Your Inbox Every Monday

Enter your email address to receive notifications of new posts, prayers and prophetic declarations sent to you by email.

Email Address

Sign Me Up

*Go to: **www.BreakThroughPrayers.org** to subscribe to receive FREE WEEKLY PRAYER POINTS, and prophetic declarations sent to you by email.*

FREE BOOKS

Download these four powerful books today for free... take your relationship with God to a new level.

www.betterlifeworld.org/grow

HOW TO USE THIS BOOK

"Without help, debts can silently prevent anyone from fulfilling their God-given assignments."

God spoke to me in 1998 to write down the things He shows me in His Word, that in time, He would use them to set the captives free. I was twenty-one years old then, and that was when I started writing down whatever God showed me in His Word, visions, and dreams.

To the glory of God, we have received thousands of testimonies of salvation, deliverance, and mysterious divine encounters through the books we publish and send out to the world.

So writing is a divine mandate for me. The purpose of this book is, therefore, not different from the central vision for which I write: *To see people set free by the power of God.*

To get the best out of this book, dedicate five days to read it, meditate on the word, and pray the prayers. Then come back and repeat the process again and again until there is a release in your spirit regarding any debt currently causing you pain. But more importantly, decide to take any action and implement any changes the Holy Spirit convicts you about.

Read the daily teachings every night and pray them before you go to bed. Or you may wake up in the middle of the night or early morning and read and pray with the book. As you do, expect an encounter with God.

INTRODUCTION

"Good day. I need prayers urgently for God to intervene in my situation. I obtained a loan from various financial institutions and have been mandated to pay by the end of this month. I don't have a dime to pay back. Failure to pay will attract a penalty through legal means. Please come to my rescue. Thank you." – Mr. John

"I am asking for guidance and strength that I will be able to close big-ticket size of clients so that I will be able to pay all my debts and will be able to support the needs of my parents and my family and that I can also share what I have to the needy." - Elis

"Good day, please pray with me for a financial breakthrough to pay all my debts this month end, in Jesus name, Amen." – Mrs. Pat

Please pray for me not to lose the house, because the water and electricity, plus house bills are in arrears. I can't afford to pay due to my high debts and little salary. Pray that if I manage to settle the debts on the house, I will be able to feed... Amen - Jayson

---

These are only four out of hundreds of prayer requests we get on our website every day. I changed the names of the requesters to keep them anonymous. But I can assure you that out of about 2,267 prayer requests posted to us in the last one-year plus, over 55% of them deal with money, with about 26% specifically on debts.

No doubt, debt is something that seriously troubles the world. And Christians are also stumbling on it. Without help, debts can silently prevent anyone from fulfilling their God-given assignments.

What keeps us in debt? What does God say about debt? How can we correctly pray our ways out of debts? And what should we do to be free from debts?

This book is written to provide you with God's wisdom and prayers for breaking free from debt. As you read and prayerfully apply the secrets revealed in this book, you will find help with any and every debt currently giving you sleepless nights.

"Debt is something that seriously troubles the world. And Christians are also stumbling on it."

---

(1): WHY YOU'RE IN DEBT

"Debt is like a coal of fire; you cannot carry it in your hands without getting hurt."

No one likes to be in debt. At least, out of every hundred debtors, I believe that about 80% do not wish to have the burden of debt in their necks. Unfortunately, that's not the situation in our world today.

I was preaching in a congregation some time ago when I suddenly decided to do a test. I asked the audience, "Is there anyone here who likes to be in debt?"

There was none.

"Okay," I went on, "Is there anyone here who is currently in some sort of debt and wants to be free?"

Almost every hand went up. Okay, let's say about 80% of the audience.

Yes, that survey is not enough to make a general conclusion, but it was enough for me to accept the reality that debt is something that many people are struggling with. And unfortunately, with little or no headway. It seems that we can't live without owing here and there.

To make progress in coming out of debt, the first question one must ask is, *"why am I in debt?"*

Below are some reasons I believe we go into debt in the first place. There may be many others, but these basics will get us started on the right course towards deliverance from debts. We must review these causes of debt and start changing our mindsets from now onwards.

1. DEBT-DRIVEN FINANCIAL SYSTEM

One reason most of us are caught up in debt is because our world's financial system is built to encourage debt slavery. As I said in my book, *Deliverance By Fire,* "You're not in debt because you're not rich."

"Think about it. Those who are rich are also in debt."

The truth is that if you had more money, you're likely to still be in debt - and even more debt - because your cost of living will always increase to match your income.

In fact, the cost of living always increase ahead of income. So while income is yet to grow, the cost of living has risen, waiting for income to come up and meet it where it is. And when income struggles and catches up, the cost of living runs upwards again.

In the end, it's always income that is struggling to catch up.

My point is that you're not in debt simply because you don't have enough money. Yes, *you can be broke and not be in debt, and you can have money and still be in debt.*

So don't only make it so much about your income and how much you earn. You must wilfully start resisting the world's financial system that is configured to keep you in debt. It's a mind game, and you must begin to play it right.

The system says, "hey, debt is a tool. Look at the benefits, not the cost. You can enjoy every good thing you want now and pay later. In fact, come and borrow more money."

Then you read finance books, and they say, "You need leverage. Learn to use *Other People's Money* to get what you want."

Then the banks add, "We'll give you a loan. You don't need to use your money. Just sign here. Take our credit cards; you can use them any time; we'll wait when you have money, so can we take what you owe us."

The real estate companies approach you and say, "Don't miss this property. Don't worry; pay us slowly and progressively, when you can."

Then we read the news and hear that even our governments owe billions and billions of dollars.

With all that war in place, we're somehow sold that it's kinda cool to borrow, borrow, and borrow some more. Our minds tell us:

- If we can have a good lifestyle now and pay later, why not?
- Can we really live without owing?
- It's not easy to live without debt. After all, everyone is owing, even the government.

So we now buy these *debt* benefits wholly because it satisfies our immediate pleasure. Why? Because we've been sold on a lie. We grew with it; we read books that encouraged it and meet counselors that sell it every minute.

Consequently, life starts replaying the results of this distortion, and before we know it, our debts keep piling up. Sadly, no one tells us that debt can keep us in a worry trap for a very long time. No one tells us that debt can even cost one's life.

> **"To get out of debt, you have to start by reprogramming your mind."**

You have to start by convincing yourself that you can live without debt and borrowing; that you would better be a lender than a debtor.

Let me put it more clearly: You need to examine what you believe about debt. If you think that debt is okay, after all, everyone owes, then you've bought the world's failed financial mind game. It doesn't matter how many times you pray and fast, you'll continually find yourself in debt.

You need to change this mindset. You can live without debt. That's how God wants you to live.

2. LACK OF CONTENTMENT

Before I got married, I called my wife to be and said, *"We must be contented with what we have at every point in time."* I told her that even if it means wearing one pair of shoes for one year, we are going to stay out of personal, lifestyle debt. I learned this from God's servant, David Oyedepo.

My wife agreed, and we prayed about it. But to be honest, it has not been comfortable sticking to this agreement.

Of course, it's always easy to make a promise; keeping it is the difference between positive results and mere emotional expression.

A lot of people make promises every new year. They get emotional and make all sorts of promises:

- I'm going to exercise every day this year
- I'm going to eat only fruits this year
- I'm going to pray for one hour every day.
- I will not go into debt again
- I will love more this year.

Unfortunately, only very few keep their promises.

Saying what you want to do is great; doing it is the key to getting the benefits.

Yes, my wife and I have failed in that promise a couple of times, but every now and then, we realize that we have missed it, repent and remind ourselves that's the way we want to live.

As long as you're alive, you're going to always have that temptation, and sometimes threat, to meet up with others, to look better than you're actually worth, and to compare yourself with someone else. If you don't fight that desire, you'll find yourself always in debt.

If I have learned anything in life, it is that there is always something better than the one I own at the moment. There's always a better TV; there's always a better suit; there's always a better washing machine, a better car; in fact, there's always a better everything. But I don't have to have them right now. I can enjoy the ones I have today while working my way up in life.

As someone said, *"life is in phases, and men are in sizes."* Enjoy what you have and can afford today. You don't have to get the ones better than your neighbor's, neither do you have to acquire the latest ones advertised on TV. You are not in competition with anyone. Don't let sales people convice you that you need something that you cant afford.

You don't have to move into a new and better apartment just because you believe that's what befits you. If you cannot afford it, then make do with what you have at the moment. Don't claim faith and leave wisdom behind.

The Bible says,

> But godliness with contentment is great gain. For we brought nothing into this world, and it is certain we can carry nothing out. And having food and raiment let us be therewith content" (1 Tim. 6:6-8).

So first things first, make up your mind to be contented with what you have. And believe me, you have a lot more than you can imagine.

Always remember, *"if you're still trying to please people, you're not Christ's servant (Galatians 1:10)."*

The Apostle Paul also said,

> Do not put yourself in the same class with or compare yourself to those who are bold enough to make their own commendations. For when they measure themselves by themselves and compare themselves to themselves, they show how foolish they are - 2 Cor. 10:12.

A good rule that will help you is this: ***"If you can't afford it, then it's not time to get it."*** Although this is not easy to practice, but you'll find out that some delayed gratification can save you of years of stress and other health problems arising from living beyond your means at the moment.

Someone said, "Some debts are fun when you are acquiring them, but none are fun when you set about retiring them."

3. POOR FINANCIAL DECISIONS

In all my years as a minister, the biggest obstacle to deliverance and breakthrough that I have seen with people is not the devil, not curses, and not lack of faith and positive confession. It is the inability to take responsibility.

When people come for prayers or come for one form of help or the other, they usually blame everyone else but themselves. When they tell their situations, it's all about how the devil, some evil people, or even their partners have hurt them really bad. There's usually little or nothing said about what they did to open the doors for the wrong things to happen.

A woman who comes for help with issues in her home would more often than not blame demons or her husband for all the problems. A man who comes for prayer for business breakthroughs will always tell you how hardworking he is, but how the wife or some demons from somewhere would not let him.

Someone who comes for deliverance from some attacks will always tell you that they haven't done anything, that they are just victims of the wicked judgments of the devil and his human agents.

I'm always carried away with compassion and tears when people tell their problems. But over the years, God has brought two scriptures to my mind. The first scripture is Proverbs 20:6, which says that *"Most men will proclaim every one his own goodness: but a faithful man who can find?"*

Everyone always tells their good part, but if they had been good and faithful as they thought, they would not have had the issues they are complaining about.

The second scripture is even more indicting. Psalm 119:67, and it says, *"Before I was afflicted, I went astray: but now have I kept thy word."*

These two scriptures informed and empowered me to help others better. Today, I don't just start praying, begging God, and binding the devil immediately someone shares their story. My first response is always, *"let's find out where you missed it."*

Nothing just happens on its own. We need to discover what we did that opened the door for something to happen; then, we can better obtain mercy from God and discern the changes we must make to move forward.

A senior minister put it this way, *"you must discover to recover."*

It is easy to blame the devil and others, but until we take responsibility and then humbly and prayerfully adjust, we may never obtain the deliverance that we seek.

It does not matter how many people you consult to pray for you; you must first and foremost find out where you missed it and then take responsibility, repent and begin to make necessary changes, even if it is gradual. Only then will deliverance take place.

Most debts and financial problems we find ourselves in, and I mean most of them, maybe not all, but most of them are a direct result of our poor judgments, poor choices, mistakes, and bad financial decisions. We must take responsibility and prayerfully begin to discern the changes we must make to obtain deliverance.

Some people spend money they have not earned, money that is not yet in their accounts. Just because they are expecting to make a sale, or hoping that someone is going to credit their accounts, they start buying things and spending from the money that is still in the air. Before you say jack, they pile up so many debts on their necks.

Some go into investments that they don't know much about. Just because someone says they could earn 100% back in a month, they gather their entire savings and put into such ventures without critical study and analysis of the business. And before you know it, they are crying about losses and debt.

Please examine yourself. That's what the Bible says. Why are you in debt? What did you do wrong? What wrong decisions and choices did you make? Have you discovered your mistakes? That's the first step to deliverance from debts.

If you don't realize why you're in debt and someone comes and helps you out just like that, you might fall back into the same debts again.

So again, take responsibility and quit blaming others. Come to terms with the reality that you did something that led to this. Then decide to make amends and start gradually.

4. UNFORESEEN CIRCUMSTANCES

There are also times that forces outside one's control can be responsible for their debt. For example, in medical emergencies, accidents, sudden failed business, or disappointments from others. However, even though we do not have direct control over these circumstances, they are only but a tiny fraction of what can keep us in debt.

According to research, these unforeseen factors only have a 30% chance of being responsible for our debts. That means that if we take care of the foreseen factors, the unforeseen factors will take care of themselves.

So yes, while it's not easy to predict how your health could change in the future *(actually, you can predict your future health situation by faith and a healthy lifestyle)*, or whether you'll lose your job or not, or whether someone you are doing business with will disappoint you or not, certain safeguards can help mitigate such risks. This is where insurance policies come in.

While the premiums we pay to keep insurance policies may seem expensive, facing these unforeseen circumstances without them in place can be very shattering.

I like to see insurance as saving for the time of famine. Even though we are a people of faith, the Bible asks us to add character and wisdom to our faith.

And beside this, giving all diligence, add to your faith virtue; and to virtue knowledge – 2Pet. 1:5

Faith without character and wisdom can lead to frustration.

When Joseph gave the plan to save Egypt from famine, they were commanded to save ahead. Yes, God has the power to make the years of abundance not to stop, but He allowed times and seasons to prevail.

In life, we will always experience times and seasons. There will always come times of plenty and times of change, times that you have a job, and times you're out of a job, times that things seem stable and times that things look very bad. What we do during times of stability is what will determine what we will see during times of instability.

If what you do is only make confessions of faith without planning for the future, you may eventually get frustrated during times of change. Add to your faith character (virtue) and wisdom. Buy into programs that develop your mind, help you save, and grow while standing in faith.

PRAYERS

Heavenly Father,

I thank You for the revelation of Your Word on debt. I humbly accept what the scriptures say and ask for the grace to walk in the light of Thy Word, in Jesus name.

Father,

Forgive me for the times I chose borrowing and debt without recourse to how You want us to live. I let my desires, haste, and ignorance overshadow Your eternal Word.

Father, forgive me.

Forgive me for every debt I ignorantly incurred on myself and on my family; forgive me for the times I let myself go into debts for lack of contentment; forgive me for the times my poor financial choices caused me to enter into debt.

By Your mercy, LORD, restore me to Your original plans henceforth, in Jesus name.

O LORD, I make a decree today against the bondage of debt.

I will no longer be held and tortured by any form of debt, in the name of Jesus Christ.

Father, I surrender myself to Your revealed financial system. From this day forward, I refuse to be controlled by the financial system of this world.

I refuse to accept borrowing and any form of debt as leverage.

You created me to be a lender and not a borrower. This, I accept in its entirety, in Jesus name.

I pray today, Father, deliver me from any form of greed and lack of contentment that continues to speak against me in the spirit.

Empower my thoughts and enable my actions to bring glory to You every day of my life.

Cause me, by the Holy Spirit, to make financial decisions that agree with Your

Word from this day forward, in the name of Jesus Christ.

O LORD, I decree that I will not be a victim of debt caused by sickness, force majeure, accidents, death, or disappointments.

Today, I take authority against every evil arrow projected from the pit of hell, or projected by wicked individuals against my health, against my finances, against my career, and against my home. I command them to be destroyed by fire this moment, in the name of Jesus Christ.

I decree today, according to God's Word, that I am walking in divine health.

I shall not die but live to declare the goodness of God.

I am like a tree planted by the riverside; whatever I lay my hands shall prosper.

As the house of Potiphar was blessed because of the presence of Joseph, so will everyone I do business or work with be blessed because of me, in Jesus name.

Henceforth, I declare that I chose to live a debt-free life.

O Lord, give me the wisdom and power to resist debts from today onwards, in Jesus name.

Amen.

"Nothing just happens on its own. We need to discover what we did that opened the door for something to happen; then, we can better obtain mercy from God and discern the changes we must make to move forward."

---

(2): THE PARABLE OF THE DEBTOR AND THE CREDITOR

"The rich rule over the poor, and the borrower is a slave to the lender." – Prov. 22:7

If you want to be delivered from debts quickly, start by changing your mindset about debt. Give up those worldly ideas and thoughts regarding debt. Accept God's perspective on debt and borrowing.

The world's financial system says, "Borrowing and debt are great, you need the leverage." But God says, *"A debtor is a slave. Owe no man anything, except to love one another..."*

You can decide to say, *"Okay, God, I go with your thoughts,"* or you can continue thinking,

"Well, everyone owes. So what's there! We can't live without owing."

Your choice is the first step towards deliverance from debt. Which option do you genuinely accept? Until you decide this mind game correctly, your war on personal debt will remain a mirage.

"Yes, God didn't say that a debtor is a sinner. But a debtor is a slave. And that's not a good thing to be."

You wouldn't want your child to be a slave, would you?

Jesus said, *", Or what man is there of you, whom if his son asks bread, will he give him a stone? ₁₀Or if he asks a fish, will he give him a serpent?₁₁ If ye then, being evil, know how to give good gifts unto your children, how much more shall your Father which is in heaven give good things to them that ask him?"* (**Matt. 7:9-11**)

Every parent wants something good for their child. I doubt there's any parent in their right senses who would opt for their children to become slaves.

A slave is a person who is legally the property of another and is forced to obey their owners. Slaves work excessively hard to keep their owners impressed. They are not entitled to vacation, breaks, and enjoyable life. That's a horrible way to live.

And the Bible says that a debtor is a slave to the creditor. Isn't that interesting? Debt confers on someone a slavery status? When its problems start coming, it can make you work excessively hard without reaping any personal benefit in your efforts.

Arise and reject debts and owing in your spirit this moment. God delivered you from every form of slavery through the death of Jesus Christ on the Cross. Don't make yourself a slave by choice through debt.

THE PARABLE OF THE DEBTOR

In Matthew chapter 18 vs. 23 – 35, Jesus told a significant parable to teach forgiveness. It is called the parable of the unmerciful servant. But I chose to call it the *Parable of the Debtor and His Creditor*.

In the parable, Jesus likened our sins to debts and proceeded to instruct us through the parable on how we will be treated when we forgive, and when we don't forgive. However, this parable also contains wisdom for dealing with debts – the very physical situation used in the parable.

These lessons, if understood, will help you deal with debts very quickly.

1. THE CREDITOR WILL ASK FOR HIS MONEY SOMEDAY

"Therefore, the Kingdom of Heaven can be compared to a king who decided to bring his accounts up to date with servants who had borrowed money from him. – Vs. 23 (NLT)

The person or entity that you owe will, one day, balance their accounts and need their money. They will come and ask for what you owe them. Have that in mind.

So even if it seems they are not disturbing at the moment, be aware that they will, someday. Therefore, make plans to repay before they ask, because they may ask for their money the way it will affect your peace of mind.

I believe in miracles, and I believe that God can touch the hearts of your creditors to cancel your debts. And I have seen this type of miracle many times. But it should not be the first thing you think concerning your debts.

Psalm 37:21 says, *"The wicked borrows and does not repay, but the righteous shows mercy and gives."*

"Only a wicked person hates to repay their debts."

Yes, our legal system allows individuals and businesses in suffering to recuperate themselves under the protection of bankruptcy laws. Unfortunately, this does not apply in all cases. And as believers, we have an obligation to repay our creditors to the best of our ability.

So make efforts to repay your debts. Pray for God's help and provision, but make efforts towards repayment.

2. YOUR DEBTS AFFECTS YOUR FAMILY

In the process, one of his debtors was brought in who owed him millions of dollars. He couldn't pay, so his master ordered that he be sold—along with his wife, his children, and everything he owned—to pay the debt. – Vs. 24-25 (NLT)

Notice that the consequences of this man's debts were also stretched to his family. The creditor's punishment also extended to the wife and children, who probably wasn't even aware of these debts.

Your debts can affect your family and generation. They do not end with you alone. So think about the stress you could be putting your family through as a result of lingering debts.

The Bible tells the story of a very good and godly prophet who died in debt. He was a good man, but he died in debt. He was godly and righteous, but he didn't have the wisdom to deal with his debts.

Unfortunately, after his death, his creditors didn't give up. They came to take his two innocent sons as collateral. But for the timely action of his wife, his innocent children would have suffered a lot (See 2 Kings 4:1-7).

As someone who has been through a terrible experience with debts, I can tell you that the pressure and stress that debts invite upon us is not what God wants us to live with. So think about the suffering you may bring upon your family through debts. It may not be today, but definitely, at some point in life.

3. FACE YOUR MESS

"But the man fell down before his master and begged him, 'Please, be patient with me, and I will pay it all.
– Vs. 26' (NLT)

Even though this parable calls this servant an *unmerciful servant*, there was one good thing he did: He faced his mess and didn't run away from his situation. He took responsibility when he was confronted with his debt. He did not look for who to blame; neither did he try to manufacture some lies and excuses to present to the creditor. Though he ended poorly, he actually started well.

In dealing with your debt and creditors, you will be tempted to protect yourself with lies and deceit many times. Unfortunately, any relief you get through lies will not last.

Don't try to play smart with those you owe. Don't try to outwit them with some false stories and fabrications.

As I often say, *"Don't try to cover, in your own way, the shame that the Lord has not covered."* If you do, it will come back in other ways, multiplied - either now or later.

Face your mess and look up to God for help. Always remember that God does not work in lies and deceits.

You can never lie your way out. Stand in truth, and God will see your humility and move the hearts of the parties involved.

When our forex investment business failed, and we ran into huge debts, our creditors dragged us to many different places. It wasn't easy. We faced a lot of shame and attacks.

But thankfully, we never missed a meeting with them. There were all kinds of threats here and there. But we gently and prayerfully followed through with everything. When many of them saw that we didn't defraud them, they started to calm down and began to pray for us.

Yes, you can pray for debt cancellation and plead for God's intervention, but while you're doing that, don't try to act fraudulently by avoiding your creditors. Face the situation with confidence that God will make a way somehow.

4. PRAYERFULLY NEGOTIATE WITH YOUR CREDITORS

26 "But the man fell down before his master and begged him, 'Please, be patient with me, and I will pay it all.' 27 Then his master was filled with pity for him, and he released him and forgave his debt. – Vs. 26-27 (NLT)

The servant in this parable begged his boss (and creditor) for total debt cancellation, and got it. The lesson here is that we can discuss with those we owe about some kind of forgiveness.

You can ask for a soft landing, or for a partial or even full debt cancellation; you can ask for a lower interest rate, more time, or more flexibility. Don't just keep quiet and do nothing in silence. Negotiate. Negotiate. Negotiate.

Let your creditors know you're doing your best. Demand forgiveness of some sort. Many will oblige when they see you honestly want to do something about the debt.

5. RECOGNIZE HABITS THAT PUT YOU IN DEBT

"But when the man left the king, he went to a fellow servant who owed him a few thousand dollars. He grabbed him by the throat and demanded instant payment. – Vs. 28 (NLT)

This servant had an unforgiving attitude, and He was also a greedy person. I can almost tell that his bad money habits were what landed him into such debts.

How is a servant under someone's payroll able to owe millions of dollars in debt (Vs.24-25 – NLT)? Did he make some investments that failed? What business did he invest in? What did he do with the monies he was borrowing from his master incessantly?

The answers to these questions are straightforward. It is almost sure he didn't invest the money in a business. Considering that he was a servant and still owed that much suggests that he was given to frivolities, gambling, get-rich-quick schemes, gluttony, fantasies, and pleasures. Those were the things that took the money.

Bad money habits, such as:

- Spending more than you earn,
- Depending on credit cards,

- Funding the good life on credit,
- Using payday loans to fund convenience,
- Continually going after get-rich-quick schemes,
- Not knowing where your money goes,
- Gambling nonstop,
- Always hoping to start saving at a later time, etc.

These habits can finish any millions and make a person go broke. And I believe those were the things that made this servant borrow so much with nothing to show for it.

"Prayerfully review and begin to deal with habits that lead to debts."

Review all your past and present money activities. Then decide to correct every action that keeps you in debt.

Often, we go into debts when we want things and lifestyles that we can't afford at the moment. We may believe that we desperately need those things and then go into debt. But the truth is that if we looked deeper, we didn't need them. There were alternatives (God's ways of escape) that we ignored.

6. FORGIVE DEBTS OWED YOU

His fellow servant fell down before him and begged for a little more time. 'Be patient with me, and I will pay it,' he pleaded. But his creditor wouldn't wait. He had the man arrested and put in prison until the debt could be paid in full. (Vs. 29-30 NLT)

Isn't this servant unbelievable? He owed someone else millions of dollars; he begged and was forgiven. Yet he couldn't forgive someone who owed him a few thousand dollars.

This entire parable teaches us forgiveness. It teaches us to remember that every time we think that someone offended us in a great way and refuses to forgive, we should not forget that God forgave our sins, which, if counted, deserved a harsher punishment.

But in our context, this also means to forgive debts that others owe us. Because the servant did not let go of the smaller debt he was owed, his master rearrested and jailed him and his family.

"If someone owing you money is unable to repay, and in all honesty, you can see that he is not able, forgive."

You will meet people like that from time to time in your life. They borrow money or do business with you and then can't pay when due. Always give the gift of forgiveness in such situations, as much as you can.

This doesn't mean you should be taken for a ride by debtors in your business because you're a Christian. Not at all.

Notice that the servant asked for his money. His action was not condemned because he asked for his money, but because even when he saw that the fellow owing him could not pay, was genuine, and has shown enough remorse, he still gave him up to be punished.

So you should ask for your money. But when you know the obvious, willingly give the gift of forgiveness. Doing this does not make you a fool. Instead, by extending mercy, you will obtain mercy in your matters when the time comes.

7. PRAY

"But the man fell down before his master and begged him, 'Please, be patient with me, and I will pay it all.' Then his master was filled with pity for him, and he released him and forgave his debt. Vs. 26-27

There are two ways to see what this servant's reaction implies. The first is to negotiate with your creditor. I have talked about this above. And the second is to pray.

Remember that, spiritually speaking, the master in this parable refers to our Father in Heaven, the Almighty God. So we can tell God about our debts.

List out all your debts in a paper and take them to the Lord. Take responsibility and ask for His mercy and forgiveness.

Ask God for help with any habit or attitude that led you to those debts. Plead the Blood of Jesus Christ, and ask God for help with the debts.

Debt is a yoke and a weight that tries to keep us down. And God can give us rest from our yokes as we come to Him in faith through Jesus Christ.

Remember that sometimes God's help with your debts may not necessarily be about canceling the debts, but about opening doors of new jobs for you so that you can earn more money to be able to pay. Sometimes His miracles can come as new business ideas. Sometimes it can come as sudden jobs or contracts that put more money in your hands.

Be open when you're praying and tell God you want a way out of your debts. Don't insist He must cancel the debts because He already says you should repay your debts.

Commit yourself to stay with God's words on money and not the sophisticated financial system of this world. God wants us to be the lenders and not the debtors. So stop borrowing and stop going into more debts.

PRAYERS

Heavenly Father,

I thank You once again for the knowledge which I receive through Your Word. Help me to be a doer of the Word and not a hearer or reader alone, in Jesus name.

I pray today, LORD, that You remind me of any debt that I have to repay. You said that only a wicked person borrows and does not want to pay back.

Father, I do not want to be this kind of person. Have mercy on me for times that I nurtured this kind of thought in the past, in Jesus name.

Today, O Lord, by the Blood of Jesus Christ, stop every form of attack, setback, and slavery I invited on my family as a result of debt.

May God's mercy and the Blood of Jesus Christ close every door that I have opened in my family spiritually, which has enabled the devil and his demons to attack us in any way, in Jesus name.

O LORD, I will not hide or run away from my debts again. Give me the wisdom and courage to face my creditors without using false stories and lies. Help me to ask for their forgiveness and assistance with the faith of getting the right response.

Father, Your word says that the heart of a king is in your hands and that You turn it wherever you will. Please set the hearts of my creditors to my favor. Speak on my behalf to them whenever I talk to them about my debt, in Jesus name.

O LORD, deliver me from every habit that has led me into debt. Show me things I do that are responsible for financial pressure in my life and family, and help me to amend my ways, in the name of Jesus Christ.

Father, help me to forgive debts owed me by others. Help me to extend Your love and mercy to anyone who genuinely needs it through me from now onwards, in the name of Jesus Christ.

O LORD, help me to recognize and take advantage of the ways of escape that you have provided for me over my debts, in Jesus name.

I bind every spirit of debt and borrowing, and cast them out of my life and family, into the abyss, in Jesus name.

I ask today, O LORD, that You give me new business ideas, opportunities, and jobs that will help me earn more so that I can pay my debts.

Thank You, LORD, for answering my prayers, in the name of Jesus Christ.

"Debt confers on someone a slavery status? When its problems start coming, it can make you work excessively hard without reaping any personal benefit in your efforts."

---

(3) WISDOM TO STAY OUT OF DEBT

"So don't worry about tomorrow, for tomorrow will bring its worries. Today's trouble is enough for today." –

Matt. 6:34 (NLT)

Every day has its troubles. Jesus wants us to live our lives on day by day basis. You can plan, yes. But you are not permitted to worry about the plans. Pray, believe, and be fine.

Unfortunately, debt brings future problems on today and increase the pains we go through. When you are in debt, you'll not be able to focus on the joy and victory that each day brings. And this is not the kind of life that Christ wants us to live.

If you're going to stay out debt, here are more scriptural instructions to meditate with and pray.

1. DON'T BE IN A HASTE TO SIGN A GUARANTEE FOR SOMEONE

Even though there's no hint from our *parable of the debtor and his creditor* that the servant signed agreements for other people who eventually defaulted and he had to pay back, I am wondering why a servant under someone's payroll could owe as much as a million dollars and more. The man, no doubt, made all the financial mistakes in his day, one of which is standing as a guarantor for others without proper knowledge.

Signing as a guarantor for someone without due diligence can get you into financial trouble. When you sign as a guarantor for anyone, what you are saying is this: "I will pay if there's any problem." And while there's nothing wrong with that, it is important to be wise when doing it.

The Bible says, *"Be sure you know a person well before you vouch for his credit! Better refuse than suffer later. Unless you have the extra cash on hand, don't countersign a note. Why risk everything you own? They'll even take your bed!"* (Proverbs 11:15, 22:26-27 - TLB).

2. BE FAITHFUL WITH EVERY LITTLE MONEY YOU HAVE

Don't wait for big-ticket sales before you give your tithe, save, and make plans. Deliver yourself from the mentality that, "Oh! This isn't enough. I'll start this financial planning program when I earn more money."

There is no better time to start whatever will improve your life than now. The only time recognized by God for decision is now. He says, *"Today is the day of salvation."*

Jesus said:

> "He who is faithful in what is least is faithful also in much, and he who is unjust in what is least is unjust also in much.

> Therefore if you have not been faithful in the unrighteous mammon, who will commit to your trust the true riches?" (Luke 16:10-11)

The wise man saves for the future, but the foolish man spends whatever he gets (Prov. 21:20 - TLB).

3. LEND TO OTHERS

God wants us to lend to others. Sounds like a paradox, right? First, we say a borrower is a slave to the lender. Next, we say, lend to others.

> For the Lord, your God will bless you just as He promised you; you shall lend to many nations,

but you shall not borrow; you shall reign over many nations, but they shall not reign over you (Deut. 15:6, 28:12, Matt. 5:42).

The message here is that if there's going to be anyone who will be a slave, then it shouldn't be the people in covenant with God. It shouldn't be us.

By being the lenders, we demonstrate the dominion and supremacy of God to the world. We show that God is, indeed, enough for us and does supply our needs. This way, we will attract others to enquire about our God.

4. RECOGNIZE GOD'S ESCAPE PLANS.

The Bible says in 1 Corinthians 10:13 that *"No temptation has overtaken you except such as is common to man; but God is faithful, who will not allow you to be tempted beyond what you are able, but with the temptation will also make the way of escape, that you may be able to bear it."*

As you pray and seek God for help and deliverance from debt, He will make a way of escape. First, He will give you the grace to bear the pressures, and sustain your health. Next, he will begin to open new doors for you: New business opportunities, new job offers, and new ideas.

Don't get stuck with expecting miraculous debt cancellations or expecting that your creditors will forget that you owe them money that you fail to recognize and take advantage of God's escape plans. And as soon as you begin to see these new blessings, don't forget your debts.

5. LEARN ABOUT MONEY AND INVESTMENT GOD'S WAY

All the suggestions outlined in this book are based on my experience and revelation from the Word of God. They will help you, as the Word will always work. But you owe yourself a duty to go beyond the lessons in this book and invest time to learn *How Money and Investments Work*. Read books on money, investment, savings, wealth creation, and increasing your income.

One thing I'm sure is that as you honestly pray and take divinely inspired steps towards your debts, God will make way for you.

6. EARN MORE

We often don't need a prophecy to know that when income decrease and expenses increase, we will suffer financial hardship. It's as simple as ABC. And the funny thing about life is that expenses are always increasing. Most times, it is income that is either ever static or continuously decreasing.

One of the ways to deal with debt is to increase your earning power and earn more. It's not easy, but it's something you have to learn to do.

How do you get started?

- Learn a new skill and
- Create other sources of income

Step out and begin to learn a couple of new things that can help you earn from more than one source of income. Start some side hustles even while focused on your present career. Learning to increase your income is vital to dealing with financial hardship and walking in financial breakthrough.

Remember that your expenses are not likely to decrease soon. So while you're trying to cut some costs here and there, start learning to increase income.

PRAYERS

Heavenly Father,

I ask for wisdom to relate with others in financial matters. Help me to discern human traps that come to steal, to kill, and to destroy my finances, and help me to reject them henceforth, in Jesus name.

O LORD,

Please remind me by Your Spirit to be faithful in all money matters going forward. Remind me that nothing is small before You. Teach me to be faithful in tithing, in giving, and in obeying scriptural instructions on money.

Help me, LORD, to be faithful in small things even as I expect Your blessings in every area of my life, in Jesus name.

O LORD,

I pray for the grace to be contented even while believing and working on bigger expectations for my life and family. May every seed of lust for things I can't afford at the moment, and comparison with others depart from me today.

Teach me, LORD, to remember that You are supplying all my needs according to Your riches in glory by Christ Jesus, and help me to stand against gluttony, excesses, and all forms of greed, in Jesus name.

From today onwards, I receive grace and power to lend to others, and not borrow.

I declare that I am a giver; I am a lender and not a borrower, in the name of Jesus Christ.

By the Blood of Jesus Christ,

I reject the curse and slavery of debt.

I come against any curse, burden, or negative influence that debts have imposed on my life, on my finances, and my family; I nullify them today, in Jesus name.

Every negative attachment I have with the god of mammon that is speaking against my finances, be destroyed, in Jesus name.

Blood of Jesus Christ, erase every spiritual liability and hard labor in my life, in Jesus name.

Fire from above, consume to ashes every power, every activity, every arrow, in heaven and on earth, that is preventing me from my breakthroughs.

May all evil projections against my finances be destroyed this day and forever, in the name of Jesus Christ.

By the blood of Jesus Christ,

I break every cycle of financial instability in my life; I come out of the valley of lack and constant financial frustration, in Jesus name.

"Debt brings future problems on today and increases the pains we go through. When you are in debt, you'll not be able to focus on the joy and victory that each day brings."

(4): SPEAK TO YOUR DEBTS

"Complaining and worrying about your debt won't get you out of it. You must do something about it."

If debts have become a mountain in your life, then do what Jesus said to do to mountains: speak to them. Speak to your debts in faith, and release God's power over the situation. The Bible says:

> For verily I say unto you, That whosoever shall say unto this mountain, Be thou removed, and be thou cast into the sea; and shall not doubt in his heart, but shall believe that those things which he saith shall come to pass; he shall have whatsoever he saith. – Mark 11:23

Jesus did not say to discuss the mountain or complain about it. Unfortunately, that's what we have been doing. No wonder the mountain is there looking at us.

Complaining and worrying about your debt won't get you out of it. You must do something about it, and one of the things you must do is to speak to your debts.

So arise today and begin to speak to your debts in the name of Jesus Christ. God is a merciful Father. The day you declare yourself free from debt, God also sees you as debt-free.

Decree and declare in faith, and the debts will start moving spiritually and physically.

Don't let anyone talk you out of this faith. Yes, We desire and work towards paying our debts, but God can cancel our debts too. Our part is to put our faith to work and not insist on debt cancellation. But as we decree and declare our position in Him, calling forth things that be not as though they are, the power of God can work out our freedom in the best way possible.

So let's go.

List all debts that you presently owe and all bills that need to be paid. Be specific about what you believe for. Then continue in prayer and speak to your debts.

PRAYERS

Today, O LORD,

I speak to all bills and debts present in my life right now; I speak to these debts and command them to be erased in the name of Jesus Christ.

Father, LORD, Show me the ways of escape that You have provided for me concerning these debts. Show me how you want me to go about them in Jesus name.

I receive divine help, ideas, and favor towards these debts this day.

Because the Lord, God, Almighty is turning my captivity around, I see myself totally free from them, in the name of Jesus Christ.

Father, LORD, May the hearts of everyone connected to these debts be turned to my favor.

May I find favor with everyone who has the influence to help me with these debts, in Jesus name.

I decree today that I see these debts canceled, and I declare myself, debt-free.

Yes, I declare myself debt-free.

May every burden, pain, setback, affliction, and suffering that my debts have invested in my life and family be lifted today, and may they never return, in Jesus name.

I congratulate myself because God's grace, power, favor, and love are going ahead of me, making all crooked places straight; His mercy is ahead of me, declaring me completely free from debts.

I will fulfill the purpose of God for my life. Nothing will ever stop me.

God is providing all my needs according to His riches in Glory, by Christ Jesus, in the name of Jesus Christ.

Thank You, Heavenly Father, for giving me wisdom and victory over debts, in Jesus name.

Amen.

God is a merciful Father. The day you declare yourself free from debt, God also sees you as debt-free

---

"The day you declare yourself free from debt, God also sees you as debt-free."

---

(5): FROM DEBT TO ABUNDANCE

"Never think that God does not care about your debt and financial troubles. He does. He will show up for you."

If you're reading this book, then it's most likely that you don't like the pressure that debts confer on us, or you're unhappy with debts in your life, and you want to do something about them; or you're learning how to stay out of debt in the first place so that you don't have to start struggling with its challenges.

Whatever the case is, don't forget that our God is merciful. When we pray and believe, His mercy is activated for our deliverance and restoration.

Debt is not a sin, but it's a weight. It's a burden that weighs us down and can quickly become a barrier between God and us.

God wants us to be free from debt. He wants us to live debt-free. He wants us to be lenders and not borrowers. May His grace and power be released in your life to become a global lender and no longer a borrower today.

You may be asking, "How can I move from a debtor to having abundance so that I can lend to others?"

If this is your question, then listen up: there is a supernatural method to moving from debt to abundance. Let me show you how it works. Please pay attention.

FROM DEBT TO ABUNDANCE

"₁ One day as he was preaching on the shore of Lake Gennesaret, great crowds pressed in on him to listen to the Word of God. ₂ He noticed two empty boats standing at the water's edge while the fishermen washed their nets. ₃ Stepping into one of the boats, Jesus asked Simon, its owner, to push out a little into the water, so that he could sit in the boat and speak to the crowds from there.

₄ When he had finished speaking, he said to Simon, **"Now go out where it is deeper and let down your nets, and you will catch a lot of fish!"**

₅ "Sir," Simon replied, "We worked hard all last night and didn't catch a thing. But if you say so, we'll try again."

₆ And this time their nets were so full that they began to tear! ₇ A shout for help brought their partners in the other boat, and soon both boats were filled with fish and on the verge of sinking.

8 When Simon Peter realized what had happened, he fell to his knees before Jesus and said, "Oh, sir, please leave us—I'm too much of a sinner for you to have around." 9 For he was awestruck by the size of their catch, as were the others with him.... 11 And as soon as they landed, they left everything and went with him."- Luke 5:1-10

You may know this scripture, but it's time to discover God through it. Please read that passage for at least two more times before you proceed.

First and foremost, remember that this story is not a parable. This is a real miraculous event that actually happened. While a parable is a fictional story with spiritual lessons, a miracle is something that happened and have witnesses.

I want you to pray that God will show you the mysteries in this story. They will not only empower your faith, but you will also know precisely what to do about your debt or financial situation right now.

Here were Peter and his professional colleagues – fishermen - spending all night in the sea and catching nothing. As experts in their trade, they knew that fishes are best caught in the night. That's when the waters are quiet for the fishes to swim to the surface of the water, looking for food or enjoying the serenity.

If there is anything like the law of fishing, Peter and his colleagues knew it well and applied it in their hustling. They were not some simpletons waiting for free food every day. They knew their job and did it well. Unfortunately, despite their competence and efforts, they caught nothing on this particular day.

There are times that, irrespective of our expertise and skills employed on our jobs and businesses, we may see nothing commensurate with our efforts. When you have days or months like that, don't turn to worry. Remember this story.

The ancient fishing model of business is such that the practitioners earn their income daily. If they caught fish to sell, they made money and provided for their families. If they caught nothing, there would be no money for them, and their families would be in danger of hunger. The only way to provide for their families, therefore, would be to go borrowing.

This was the situation that Peter and his friends found themselves. They caught nothing all through the night, and so there would be no money for the home upkeep. Their only option was to borrow. While washing their nets, I believe they were pondering what to do for the day. And all of a sudden, Jesus showed up.

I like to assure you that in your present financial situation, Jesus will certainly show up. Never think that God does not care about your debt and financial troubles. He does. If Jesus showed up for Peter and his friends, He will certainly show up for you.

TAKE YOUR FOCUS AWAY FROM THE PROBLEM

When Jesus came on the scene, Peter and his friends paid attention. They had heard about this former carpenter and His new movement. They had heard about his miracles, especially about healing the sick. They loved His way, and today, it was an opportunity to watch him preach and heal.

This is the first key here. Pay attention to the word of God. When you're in a financial problem, it's easy to think that you don't need God and prayers, but you do. Instead of staying away from Church and prayer, increase your attendance and service. Pray more in the spirit, praise more, and rejoice more. Your spiritual focus will determine your physical results.

Notice that when Jesus appeared on the scene, he saw their problem. He knew that these family men needed food. He knew that they had toiled all night with nothing to show for it. He saw everything.

But what did He do? He went ahead to beg Peter for His boat to preach the gospel first.

Now, don't you think that the right thing to do was to first and foremost help them with some miracle? That would have made them excited and maybe boosted their faith, right?. But no. Instead, He asked for the guy who's going through a horrible emotional problem to lend Him his boat for preaching. What kind of man is that?

I bet that some religious analysts there were offended with him for that action. They probably added it to His list of offenses, and privately continued thinking of him as one of these new-age, insensitive, unsympathetic preachers. They probably thought, "Cant this man see that these guys are hungry and need help? Instead of helping these folks, he's asking for a boat to preach."

But you see, what Jesus did here was teaching them to remove their attention from their problem and focus on the kingdom. He was simply telling them, *"Guys, I can see your frustration. But stop dwelling on it. Remove your attention from what you couldn't achieve; stop thinking of the failure, the losses, and the impending debt. Stop the fear and give God your faith."*

And that's a critical key to move from debt to abundance: *stop the fear and give God your faith.*

Take your attention away from the unfortunate past, the failures, the losses, the associates who made things worse, and the wrong decisions and choices. Kill the worries and regrets and turn to God with a new hope.

Here's how it works: you don't get the miracle so that you can stop the worry and fear, you stop the worry and fears to get the miracle.

If this point is still hard to understand, then let me put it this way, "God knows that you're in debt. He knows that you need financial breakthrough urgently. But you have to focus less on the problem and focus more on Him."

God must first work in you before He works for you. This is another way of saying that financial miracles and breakthroughs start from the inside.

"If the miracle of abundance does not take place inside you, it does not take place outside."

Anxiety will not get you anywhere. Focusing on the problem negatively will only make matters worse. You need to prayerfully come to an emotional rest, where you're less focused on the magnitude of the problem and focused on the goodness of God and His power to make way for you.

See how the Apostle Paul tells us to do this:

"So here's what I want you to do, God helping you: Take your everyday, ordinary life—your sleeping, eating, going-to-work, and walking-around life—and place it before God as an offering. Embracing what God does for you is the best thing you can do for him.

"Don't become so well-adjusted to your culture that you fit into it without even thinking. Instead, fix your attention on God. You'll be changed from the inside out. Readily recognize what he wants from you, and quickly respond to it. Unlike the culture around you, always dragging you down to its level of immaturity, God brings the best out of you, develops well-formed maturity in you." – Rom. 12:1-2 (MSG)

Give yourself to the daily pursuit of God's word through reading, hearing, meditation, and declaration. Do that nonstop to build your spirit-man.

Your mind will rebel against this pursuit in the beginning, but it will cooperate as you persist. As you do this, you will begin to discern what actions are right to take regarding your finances. God will begin to drop into your spirit-man who to talk to, what to say, how to react when spoken to about your debts, and how to connect to the doors that are already spiritually open for you.

GIVE JESUS YOUR BOAT

After getting Peter's attention, Jesus asked for his boat for His Crusade and even requested him to push out a little into the water, so that he could sit in the boat and speak to the crowds from there. What does this mean?

This is where it gets technical for modern Christians. Many preachers and writers interpret this to signify: *sow a seed, give an offering, make a financial sacrifice, and vow.*

They will add to this interpretation, Psalm 126: 5-6, which says, "Those who sow in tears shall reap in joy. He who continually goes forth weeping, bearing seed for sowing, shall doubtless come again with rejoicing, bringing his sheaves with him."

Unfortunately, interpreting Peter's giving of his boat to Christ to mean sowing a sacrificial money seed during financial challenges is not the whole truth. This is because while it is vital to sow and give even in times of famine, what Peter's boat means here is relative to individual persons.

To one believer, giving Jesus your boat may mean a vow, a seed, a sacrificial offering, while to another, it could mean something else. It must not be summed up to money giving.

I have seen many sincere Christians who have followed this stereotype over the years without experiencing any breakthrough. They give, give, and give expecting some kind of miracles to happen, but it never happens. Many have complained to me, "Pastor, I have been sowing and giving and making vows here and there, but everything continues to work against me. Everyone is saying that a harvest is coming, but that's years now. I'm going to lose my house next week; my kids are out of school ... what else should I do?"

When I hear things like that, I know that I am listening to a sincere Christian who has tried fruitlessly to change their financial predicaments through money giving. My heart bleeds for their pain.

The best way for you to find out what Peter's boat mean for you as a believer is to ask Jesus.

Sometimes what Peter's boat means for you may be your time; maybe you've been too busy with things of this world, and now God's needs your time.

Sometimes it may mean to renew your prayer altar or to give up a lifestyle that is very dear to you, but which is against your divine destiny.

Sometimes it may mean to forgive a severe offense, one that you have been struggling with, or making peace with someone.

Sometimes it may mean spending time waiting on the Lord and interceding for someone or a ministry. And sometimes, it can also mean dealing with specific strongholds, negative beliefs, and attitudes in your life.

"Don't summarize your boat to mean money. Find out from God what it is and be willing to lay it on His altar."

"Okay, Pastor, How do I know what my boat is?" You ask.

Go back to the first step. When you start focusing less on the problem and focus more on God, your heart will discern what your boat is. When you then give Him your boat, you can be sure of the next life-changing miracle.

LISTEN TO WHAT HE SAYS TO YOU

When Jesus had finished speaking, he said to Simon, *"Now go out where it is deeper and let down your nets, and you will catch a lot of fish!"*

That's what you need: *a divine instruction.*

When I was growing up in faith, I was taught that if you needed a financial breakthrough, sow money seeds. I went from place to place giving and sowing seeds. Unfortunately, I never had any reasonable breakthrough.

Thank God we survived, but I didn't get the kinds of remarkable financial breakthrough experiences the preachers said we would have if we only sowed seeds. With time, I began to ask myself what was missing. Is it that God lied, or that the preachers didn't tell the whole truth, or that I was the problem.

I eliminated the option of God a liar and was left with either the principle is not the complete truth or that I was the problem. And once I began to work on those premises, I started to see things more clearly.

My answer did not come immediately, because it takes time for God to get our attention. It takes time for God to change our thoughts from popular beliefs to His thoughts. But thankfully, I found an answer that calmed my soul.

God showed me in scriptures that the key to financial breakthrough and any miracle for that matter is hearing what He is saying and following the instruction per time. In other words, money giving is not all I needed to do to experience a financial breakthrough.

Giving should be a daily lifestyle of every believer. But beyond that, we must come to a point where we discern what the Lord is saying to us and follow it. Otherwise, we may give everything we have and still not experience any breakthrough. This is the missing link in our giving and the answer to the search for the key to financial breakthrough.

"Whatever He says to you, do it." (John 2:5)

That, right there, is the omitted key.

You are giving and sowing seeds, that's great. Excellent. Continue. But go beyond that. Ask God what He wants you to do.

Every miracle in scripture answered to someone following an instruction. The widow of Zarephath's flour did not multiply because she gave, but because she gave in response to God's instruction to her.

> Then the Lord said to him, "Go and live in the village of Zarephath, near the city of Sidon. There is a widow there who will feed you. **I have given her my instructions.**" - 1 Kings 17:8-9 (TLB)

God had instructed her about feeding Elijah. We're not told how, but God did. It could be through a dream, a trance, an angelic encounter, or whatever. The point is that God had told her ahead of time because He's not a liar.

God did not send Elijah to the widow of Zarephath before telling the widow. He sent Elijah after telling the widow. Elijah was only confirming what God had revealed to this woman

Yes, the widow argued with Elijah initially because she was human. She wanted some confirmation and assurance that what God had shown her was in order and that she was not losing her mind. When she finally decided to donate her last meal as she was instructed, the miracle of multiplication took place.

I can tell you that if I go about asking every widow in our church to give their last meals, that is, to close their account and bring all their savings to Church, just as this widow did, they may not experience instant multiplication like the widow. Same actions, different results. Why? Divine instruction.

God will undoubtedly bless all givings and financial sacrifices, but there's a difference when you are instructed and when you're not.

God can instruct you to give, to make a special vow, or sacrifice in a ministry; He can also ask you to call someone and return his property that you kept without permission. Or He can tell you to invest in a particular business, or resign from your present job and start another one.

Let Him show you what you must do. And whatever He says to you, do it. Don't only make God's instruction for your prosperity and breakthrough about money giving.

One thing about divine instruction is that even when you are doing it doubtfully, the results still come back as miracles. God knows that our minds do not understand the depth of His ways. So He does not stop the results because we doubted and feared.

The question every believer should continually ask is, "God, what are you saying to me about this situation?" The answer is what breaks every spiritual barrier, opens every door, and commands an unfathomable financial harvest.

EVEN IF YOU'RE NOT SURE, TRY IT

When Jesus gave Peter the instruction of what to do, he said, "Sir, we worked hard all night and didn't catch a thing. But if you say so, we'll try again."

In other words, "Jesus, this is not a good time to throw the net into the sea. I know this job very well. That's what I do for a living. So I'm not sure any fish will be there. I'm not sure this will work. I'll rather not embarrass you and myself, but because you have said so, let me try again."

And to his greatest dismay, their nets were so full that they began to tear!

Hallelujah!

If God is telling you something, even if you're not sure how it will work out, go ahead and try it first. You say, "brother Dan, I'm not even sure God is speaking to me."

No dear, He is speaking to you. But you're not listening, or you're focused more on talking to Him than listening to Him.

You have to change your approach: **Know that God is speaking to you you.** That's the first step to hearing His voice. Then clear your mind of too many distractions. Switch off your phone and turn off social media for some time. Get some seclusion and listen. The instruction you need will be right there waiting.

Notice that Peter was not too sure what would happen, but he decided to try anyway, and his life changed. The widow of Zarephath was also not too sure if anything would happen, but she chose to obey the instruction she received. Her life changed, and she and her son were preserved.

Everything written in scripture is for our learning so that we will be instructed unto righteousness – doing the right thing. God's ways have not changed. The same power that multiplied the widow's flour and delivered a net breaking harvest of fishes is still available today. Align yourself with His ways, and command His acts.

Your financial miracle is right there with you. Take it now. If you do, it will be the beginning of your experience of His abundance. Then you will move from a debtor to a lender.

PRAYERS

Heavenly Father, I pray today for divine rest. Calm my fears and worries about my finances and help me to focus more on You. Deliver me from all forms of distractions that keep me far away from Your presence, in Jesus name.

O LORD, I ask that You baptize me with the spirit of praise, joy, and worship. Help me to rejoice in you no matter the situation physically.

Empower my faith and cause my spirit to be peaceful and trust in Your unchanging promises, in the name of Jesus Christ.

O LORD, You showed up for Peter and his friends and turned their frustration into a marvelous harvest of breakthrough. You're the same, yesterday, today, and forever.

I, therefore, pray now, LORD, show up for me. Let every worry and fear in my life today be turned into a great harvest of breakthrough, in the name of Jesus Christ.

Heavenly Father, You know all my needs, and You have promised to supply all my needs according to Your riches in Christ Jesus.

Today, I remind You to bless me financially.

Let the doors of heaven be open unto me from this day forward and cause me to walk in Your prosperity and abundance, in Jesus name.

Show me, O LORD, what my boat represents today. I confess that I am willing to lay whatever it is on Your altar. Only open my eyes and show me what has to leave me for Your blessings to locate me in Jesus name.

Heavenly Father, open my ears and cause me to hear clearly what You are saying to me to do about my finances from now onwards. If you want me to talk to someone, LORD, show me. If you want me to invest somewhere, LORD, show me. If you want me to leave somewhere and go somewhere else, please LORD, show me.

Give me a clear direction to follow from today, in the name of Jesus Christ.

I take authority in the name of Jesus Christ and bind the spirits of distraction, confusion, fear, and carelessness. I decree that I will no longer walk in darkness concerning my finances in Jesus name.

O LORD, help me to obey Your instructions and ideas even when they don't make sense physically, for I know that obedience is the key to taking delivery of Your promises, in Jesus name.

As I close my eyes this moment, I see abundance and supernatural open doors. Yes, I receive financial abundance into my life and family this moment in Jesus name.

I call forth financial abundance into my life this moment.

Financial abundance, come forth now.

Angels of money, go now and connect me with anyone connected to my financial breakthrough.

I declare my barns, my house, and my bank account filled and overflowing with supernatural provisions henceforth.

I see myself giving and distributing to others from God's abundance in my care, in Jesus name.

"Pay attention to the word of God. When you're in a financial problem, it's easy to think that you don't need God and prayers, but you do... Pray more in the spirit, praise more, and rejoice more. Your spiritual focus will determine your physical results.

God

bless

you

GET IN TOUCH

We love testimonies. We love to hear what God is doing around the world as people draw close to Him in prayer.

If this book has blessed...Kindly check out our website at www.BetterLifeWorld.org, and drop your praise report. You can also send us your prayer request. As we join faith with you, God's power will be made manifest in your life.

Also, please consider giving this book a review on Amazon, and checking out our other titles at:

www. amazon.com/author/danielokpara.

OTHER BOOKS BY THE SAME AUTHOR

Latest Books

31 Days in the School of Faith

31 Days With the Heroes of Faith

31 Days With the Holy Spirit

31 Days With Jesus

31 Days in the Parables

None of These Diseases

I Will Arise and Shine

Psalm 91: His Secret Place, His Shadow, and His Protection

All Books

<u>Prayer Retreat:</u> 21 Days Devotional With Over 500 Prayers & Declarations to Destroy Stubborn Demonic Problems.

<u>HEALING PRAYERS & CONFESSIONS</u>

<u>200 Violent Prayers</u> for Deliverance, Healing, and Financial Breakthrough.

<u>Hearing God's Voice in Painful Moments</u>

<u>Healing Prayers:</u> Prophetic Prayers that Brings Healing

<u>Healing WORDS:</u> Daily Confessions & Declarations to Activate Your Healing.

<u>Prayers That Break Curses</u> and Spells and Release Favors and Breakthroughs.

<u>120 Powerful Night Prayers</u> That Will Change Your Life Forever.

<u>How to Pray for Your Children Everyday</u>

<u>How to Pray for Your Family</u>

<u>Daily Prayer Guide</u>

Make Him Respect You: 31 Very Important Relationship Intelligence for Women to Make their Men Respect them.

How to Cast Out Demons from Your Home, Office & Property

Praying Through the Book of Psalms

The Students' Prayer Book

How to Pray and Receive Financial Miracle

Powerful Prayers to Destroy Witchcraft Attacks.

Deliverance from Marine Spirits

Deliverance From Python Spirit

Anger Management God's Way

How God Speaks to You

Deliverance of the Mind

20 Commonly Asked Questions About Demons

Praying the Promises of God

When God Is Silent! What to Do When Prayer Seems Unanswered or Delayed

I SHALL NOT DIE: Prayers to Overcome the Spirit and Fear of Death.

Praise Warfare

Prayers to Find a Godly Spouse

How to Exercise Authority Over Sickness

Under His Shadow: Praying the Promises of God for Protection (Book 2).

Audio Books

120 Powerful Night Prayers that Will Change Your Life

28 Days of Praise Challenge: Dealing With Your Fears and Battles Through Intentional Praise

Anger Management God's Way: Bible Ways to Control Your Emotions, Get Healed of Hurts & Respond to Offenses ...Plus Powerful Daily Prayers to Overcome Bad Anger Permanently

By His Stripes: God's Promises & Prayers for Healing

Deliverance of the mind: Powerful Prayers to Deal With Mind Control, Fear, Anxiety, Depression, Anger and Other Negative Emotions.

Healing Words: Daily Confessions & Declarations to Activate Your Healing

How God Speaks to You: An ABC Guide to Hearing the Voice of God & Following His Direction for Your Life

How to Exercise Authority Over Sickness: Authoritative Prayers and Declarations for Personal Healing, and Healing of Your Loved Ones

How to Meditate on God's Word: Fast and Easy Ways to Practice Intentional Bible Meditation and Grow in Faith, Worship, and Prayer

Prayers to Find a Godly Spouse: Meditations, Prophetic Declarations and Biblical Foundation for Finding a Life Partner

Praying the Promises of God for Daily Blessings and Breakthrough

Take it By Force: 200 Violent Prayers for Deliverance, Healing and Financial Breakthrough

Under His Shadow: God's Promises and Prayers for Protection

When God Is Silent: What to Do When Prayers Seems Unanswered or Delayed

Beside the Still Waters: God's Promises and Prayers for Guidance and Direction | Learn to Know the Will of God & Make Right Decisions

Less Panic More Hope: God's Promises and Prayers to Overcome Fear, Anxiety, and Depression – Scriptures and Prayers for Mental Health

How to Pray for Your Family: Plus Over 70 Prayers for Your Family's Salvation, Healing, Restoration, and Breakthrough

Prayers that Break Curses: Everything You Need to Know About Curses, and Powerful Prayers to Stop All Kinds of Curses

20 Commonly Asked Questions About Demons: Answers You Need to Bind and Cast Out Demons, Heal the Sick, and Experience Breakthrough

Deliverance by Fire: 21 Days of Intensive Word Immersion, and Fire Prayers for Total Healing, Deliverance, Breakthrough, and Divine Intervention.

Command Your Money: Powerful Keys to Provoke Financial Breakthrough | 10 Simple Actions of Faith That Will Provoke Financial Breakthrough for Anyone in 30 Days or Less

About the Author

Daniel Chika Okpara is an influential voice in contemporary Christian ministry. His mandate is to make lives better through the teaching and preaching of God's Word with signs and wonders. He is the resident pastor of Shining Light Christian Centre, a fast-growing church in the city of Lagos.

He is also the president and CEO of Better Life World Outreach Center, a non-denominational ministry dedicated to global evangelism, prayer revival, and empowering of God's people with the WORD to make their lives better. Through his Breakthrough Prayers Foundation (www.breakthroughprayers.org), an online portal leading people all over the world to encounter God and change their lives through prayer, thousands of people encounter God through prayer, and hundreds of testimonies are received from all around the world.

As a foremost Christian teacher and author, his books are in high demand in prayer groups, Bible studies, and personal devotions. He has authored over 50 life-transforming books and manuals on business, prayer, relationship and victorious living, many of which have become international best-sellers.

He is a Computer Engineer by training and holds a Master's Degree in Christian Education from Continental Christian University. He is married to Doris Okpara, his best friend, and the most significant support in his life. They are blessed with lovely children.

WEBSITE: www.betterlifeworld.org

NOTES